Goldilocks
- What Ever Happened To Her?

To you, Beatrice Dvilnsky, illustrator of this book.
I searched for information about you. I really did.
Have you disappeared?

Gabriel Rosenstock

Published in association with
Bear With Us Productions

© 2023 Gabriel Rosenstock and
Cross-Cultural Communications
Goldilocks - What Ever happened to her?

The right of Gabriel Rosenstock and
Cross-Cultural Communications
239 Wynsum Avenue, Merrick,
NY 11566-4724 / USA as the authors of
this work has been asserted by them in
accordance with the Copyright Designs
and Patents Act 1988. All rights reserved,
including the right of reproduction in whole
or part in any form.

Design by Emma Evans
Illustrated by Beatrice Dvilnsky
www.justbearwithus.com

Written By
Gabriel Rosenstock

Goldilocks
- What Ever Happened To Her?

Illustrated By
Beatrice Dvilnsky

Who goes there?

It's Mommy Bear, Daddy Bear and Baby Bear.
They often went out for a breath of fresh air!

They lived in a wood
Where the air was quite good!

It smelled of trees
And honey and bees.

They lived a life of luxury and ease.

They loved porridge, it made them strong!
They started each day with porridge and a song:

"Porridge, porridge, full of oats,
Good for horses, good for goats.
Please spare a spoonful for poor Johnny Forty Coats!"

This was where they slept at night –
Hoping the nasty bugs wouldn't bite!

Their dreams were peaceful, often boring.
They didn't like screaming and shouting and roaring.
One morning, said Daddy, "This porridge is too hot!
Why don't we all go out for a trot?"

They liked fresh air – a lot!

They had a little trot and they had a little stroll.
Meanwhile, the porridge was cooling in the bowl!

Who came along but little Goldilocks!
She knocked and she knocked.
She knocked and she knocked.

"Hey! Hello? I'm not going to knock anymore!
Come on now! Open this donkey-dunderhead door!
My knuckles are getting sore!"

In she did go,
On her tippy-tippy toes.

She tasted the porridge – only Baby's one was nice!
"The other two porridges? Huh! I'll leave that goo to the mice!"

She was tired from walking all day in the wood.
And sat herself down, as a little girl should.

Crash! Bang! Wallop! She'd broken Baby's chair.
"Huh!" said Goldilocks. "See if I care!"

"I could sleep now," she said with a yawn.
"I could sleep until dawn."

That's what she said
As she lay down gently in Baby's bed.
"I'll rest my head . . .
Yikes! It smells like stale mouldy bread!"

"Hmm . . . something's queer!
Someone's been here!"

"Dad! Dad!" shouted Baby Bear.
"Look at my bowl! There's nothing there!
Who would eat my porridge? Who would even dare?"

"Look over there!"
screamed Mommy Bear.
"Poor Baby's chair!
Well, I declare!"

Said Daddy Bear to his precious wife,
"Never seen anything like it in my life!"

Slowly Goldilocks opened her eyes:
Three bears were glaring at her – what a surprise!

She began to cough.
"OK, Bears, I'm off!"

"This is PRIVATE PROPERTY!" roared big Daddy Bear.
"You lot! You think everything in this world is free to share!"

She ran and she ran through the private wood
As fast as she could!

Later she grew up to be a very sharp writer –
And a freedom fighter!

I THINK YOU'D LIKE HER!

www.ingramcontent.com/pod-product-compliance
Lightning Source LLC
Chambersburg PA
CBHW041326290426

44110CB00004B/153